The Haunted House
A True Ghost Story

WALTER HUBBELL

Neelkanth
Prakashan

ISBN: 978-93-6144-554-5

Publisher: Neelkanth Prakashan

Address: 4760-61, 23, Ansari Road,
Daryaganj, New Delhi-110002
Phone: 9810675061
WhatsApp: +91 9810675061
E-mail: neelkanthprakashan47@gmail.com

Edition: 2024

Printed By: Gupta Communication Shahdra 110032

The Haunted House A True Ghost Story
WALTER HUBBELL

INTRODUCTION

The manifestations described in this story commenced one year ago. No person has yet been able to ascertain their cause. Scientific men from all parts of Canada and the United States have investigated them in vain. Some people think that electricity is the principal agent; others, mesmerism; whilst others again, are sure they are produced by the devil. Of the three supposed causes, the latter is certainly the most plausible theory, for some of the manifestations are remarkably devilish in their appearance and effect. For instance, the mysterious setting of fires, the powerful shaking of the house, the loud and incessant noises and distinct knocking, as if made by invisible sledge-hammers, on the walls; also, the strange actions of the household furniture, which moves about in the broad daylight without the slightest visible cause.

As these strange things only occur while Miss Esther Cox is present, she has become known as the "Amherst Mystery" throughout the entire country.

The author of this work lived for six weeks in the haunted house, and considers it his duty to place the entire matter before the public in its true light, having been requested to do so by the family of Miss Cox.

CONTENTS

THE HAUNTED HOUSE

CHAPTER I

THE HOME OF ESTHER COX

Amherst, Nova Scotia, is a beautiful little village on the famous Bay of Fundy; has a population of about three thousand souls, and contains four churches, an academy, a music hall, a large iron foundry, a large shoe factory, and more stores of various kinds than any village of its size in the Province.

The private residences of the more wealthy inhabitants are very picturesque in their appearance, being surrounded by beautifully laid out lawns, containing ornamental trees of various kinds and numerous beds of flowers of choice and sometimes very rare varieties.

The residences of Parson Townsend, Mr. Robb, Doctor Nathan Tupper, and Mr. G.G. Bird, proprietor of the Amherst book store; also that of Mr. Amos Purdy, the village Post Master, and others too numerous to mention, are sure to attract the visitor's attention and command his admiration.

On Princess street, near Church, there stands a neat two story cottage, painted yellow. It has in front a small yard, which extends back to the stable. The tidy appearance of the cottage and its pleasant situation are sure to attract a stranger's attention. Upon entering the house everything is found to be so tastefully arranged, so scrupulously clean, and so comfortable, that the visitor feels at home in a moment, being confident that everything is looked after by a thrifty housewife.

The first floor consists of four rooms, a parlor containing a large bay window, filled with beautiful geraniums of every imaginable color and variety, is the first to attract attention; then the dining room, with its old fashioned clock, its numerous home made rugs, easy chairs, and commodious table, makes one feel like dining, especially if the hour is near twelve; for about that time of day savory odors are sure to issue from the adjoining kitchen. The kitchen is all that a room of the kind in a village cottage should be, is not very large, and contains an ordinary wood stove, a large pine table, and a small washstand, has a door opening into the side yard near the stable, and another into the wash shed, besides the one connecting it with the dining room, making three doors in all, and one window. The fourth room is very small, and is used as a sewing room; it adjoins the dining room, and the parlor, and has a door opening into each. Besides the four rooms on the first floor, there is a large pantry, having a small window about four feet from the floor, the door of this pantry opens into the dining room. Such is the arrangement of the first floor.

Upon ascending a short flight of stairs, and turning to the left, you find yourself in the second story of the cottage, which consists of an entry and four small bed rooms, all opening into the entry. Each one of the rooms has one window, and only one door. Two of these little bed rooms face towards the street, and the other two towards the back of the cottage. They, like the rest of the house, are conspicuous for their neat, cosy aspect, being papered and painted, and furnished with ordinary cottage furniture. In fact everything about the little cottage will impress a casual observer with the fact that its inmates are happy, and evidently at peace with God and man.

This humble cottage is the home of Daniel Teed, shoemaker. Everybody knows and respects honest hard working Dan, who never owes a dollar if he can help it, and never allows his family to want for any comfort that can be procured, with his hard earned salary as foreman of the Amherst Shoe Factory.

Dan's family consists of his wife Olive, as good a soul as ever lived, always hard at work. From early morning until dusky eve she is on her feet. It has always been a matter of gossip and astonishment, among the neighbors, as to how little Mrs. Teed, for she is by no means what you would call a large woman, could work so incessantly without becoming weary and resting for an hour or so after dinner. But she works on all the same, never rests, and they still look on her with astonishment. Dan and Olive have two little boys. Willie, the eldest, is **five** years old; he is a strong, healthy looking lad, with a ruddy complexion, blue eyes, and brown curly hair; his principal amusements are throwing stones, chasing the chickens, and hurting his little brother. George, the youngest of Dan's boys, is the finest boy of his age in the village and is only a little over a year old; his merry little laugh, winning ways, and cunning actions to attract attention have made him a favorite with all who visit at the cottage.

Besides his wife and two little boys, Dan has under his honest roof and protection his wife's two sisters,—Jane and Esther Cox—who board with him. Jane is a lady-like, self-possessed young woman of about twenty-two, and is quite a beauty; her hair is very light brown and reaches below her waist when she allows it to fall in graceful tresses—at other times she wears it in the Grecian style; her eyes are of a greyish hue; a clear complexion and handsome teeth add to her fine appearance. In fact, Jane Cox is one of the village belles, and has hosts of admirers, not of the male sex alone, for she is also popular among the ladies; she is a member and regular attendant of Parson Townsend's Church, which, by the way, the good Parson has had under his care for about forty-five years. Esther Cox, Dan's other sister in-law, is such a remarkable girl in every respect that I must give as complete a description of her as possible. She was born in Upper Stewiacke, Nova Scotia, on March 28th, 1860, and is consequently in her eighteenth year. Esther has always been a queer girl. When born she was so small that her good, kind grandmother, who raised her, (her mother having died when she was three weeks old) had to wash and dress her on a pillow, and in fact keep her on it all the time until she was nine months old, at which age her weight was only five pounds. When she was quite a little girl her father, Archibald T. Cox, married again, and moved to East Machias, Maine, where he has since resided. Having followed his second wife to the grave, he married a third with whom he is now living. Esther's early years having been spent with her grandmother, she very naturally became grave and old-fashioned, without knowing how or why. Like all little girls, she was remarkably susceptible to surrounding influences, and the sedate manner and actions of the old lady made an early impression on Esther that will cling to her through life.

In person Esther is of low stature and rather inclined to be stout; her hair is curly, of a dark brown color, and is now short, reaching only to her shoulders; her eyes are large and grey, with a bluish tinge, and an earnest expression which seems to say, "why do you stare at me so; I can not help it if I am not like other people." Her eye-brows and eye-lashes are dark and well marked, that is to say, the lashes are long and the eye-brows very distinct. Her face is what can be called round, with well shaped features; she has remarkably handsome teeth, and a pale complexion. Her hands and feet are small and well shaped, and although inclined to be stout, she is fond of work, and is a great help to her sister Olive, although she sometimes requires a little urging.

Although Esther is not possessed of the beauty that Jane is famous for, still there is something earnest, honest and attractive about this simple-hearted village maiden, that wins for her lots of friends of about her own age; in fact, she is quite in demand among the little children of the neighborhood also, who are ever ready to have a romp and a game with **Ester**, as they all call her. The truth is, a great many of the grown up inhabitants of the village call her **Ester** also, dropping the **h** entirely, a habit common in Nova Scotia.

Esther's disposition is naturally mild and gentle. She can at times, however, be very self-willed, and is bound to have her own way when her mind is made up. If asked to do anything she does not feel like doing she becomes very sulky and has to be humored at times to keep peace in the family. However, all things considered, she is a good little girl and has always borne a good reputation in every sense of the word.

There are two more boarders in the little cottage, who require a passing notice. They are William Cox and John Teed. William is the brother of Olive, Jane, and Esther, and is a shoemaker by trade, and one of Dan's workmen in the factory.

The other boarder, John Teed, is Dan's brother. John, like his brother, is an honest, hard working young man, has been raised a farmer, an occupation he still follows when not boarding with Dan in Amherst.

As the reader may, perhaps, be anxious to know how Dan, good, honest hard working Dan, and, his thrifty little wife Olive, look, I will endeavor to give a short description of each. So here goes. Dan is about thirty-five years old, and stands five feet eight in his stockings. He has light brown hair, rather thin on top, a well shaped head, blue eyes, well defined features, a high nose, and wears a heavy moustache and bushy side whiskers; his complexion is florid; rheumatism of several years standing has given him a slight halt in the left leg. He does his work, spends his salary as he should, and leads a Christian life, has a pew in the Wesleyan Church of which Rev. R.A. Temple is pastor, belongs to a temperance society, and, I dare say, when he dies will be well rewarded in the next world. Olive, as I have already said, is not a very large woman. She is good and honest, like her husband, and goes to church with him as a wife should. Her hair is dark brown, eyes grey, complexion pale and slightly freckled. Although not as beautiful as Jane, nor at any time as sulky as Esther can be, she has those motherly traits of character which command respect. Being older than her sisters she is looked up to by them for advice when they think they need it, and consolation when they are in sorrow. Olive's wise little head is sure to give the right advice at the right time, and in the family of the cottage her word is law. I do not mean to say that she rules her husband. No! Dan is far from being a hen-pecked man, but, as two heads are always better than one, Dan often takes her advice and profits by it.

Such is the cottage and household of honest Dan Teed.

To-day is cool and pleasant. The hour is nearly twelve noon—the hour for dinner in the cottage. Esther is seated on the parlor floor playing with George to keep him from running out in the hot sun. Willie is out in the yard near the stable tormenting a poor hen, who has had a log of wood tied to one of her legs by Olive to prevent her from setting in the cow's stall; but master Willie seems to think she has been tied so that he may have a good time banging her over the head with a small club, which he is doing in a way that means business. Suddenly his mother comes out of the kitchen, and after soundly boxing his ears, sends him howling into the house, much to the relief of the poor hen who has just fallen over with exhaustion and fright, but upon finding her tormentor gone is soon herself again. Presently Olive hears Dan at the gate, and comes to the front door to meet him and tell him that dinner is almost ready, remarking that he cannot guess what she has for dessert. Honest Dan replies that no matter what it is he is hungry and will eat it, for he has been working hard. So in he goes to wash his hands and face at the wash-stand in the kitchen.

Jane is coming down the street. Esther, who is seated on a chair with George on her lap, sees her sister from the bay window in the parlor. Jane has a position in Mr. Jas. P. Dunlap's establishment, and goes to her work every morning at seven o'clock. As soon as Esther sees Jane she takes George up in her arms and runs in to tell Olive that Jane is coming, and suggests that dinner be served at once, for **she** feels hungry. So Olive, with Esther's assistance, puts the dinner on the table, and they all sit down to enjoy the meal, and a good substantial meal it is; plenty of beef-steak and onions, plenty of hot mashed potatoes, plenty of boiled cabbage, and an abundance of home made bread and fresh butter made that very morning from the rich cream of Dan's red cow. Little George, who is seated in his high chair at his mother's right hand, commences to kick the bottom of the table in such a vigorous manner that not one word can be heard, for he makes a terrible noise, the toes of his shoes being faced with copper to prevent the youngster from wearing them out too soon. Olive asks Esther to please get the old pink scarf and tie his feet so that he will be unable to make such a racket, Esther does not move, but upon being requested a second time gets up rather reluctantly, goes to the hat rack in the hall, gets the scarf and ties the little fellow's feet, as requested. Upon reseating herself at the table it is noticeable that she has a sulky expression, for she does not like to be disturbed while enjoying dinner, nor in fact any meal, for the simple reason that her appetite is voracious, being particularly fond of pickles, and she has been known to drink a cupful of vinegar in a day.

All ate in silence for some minutes, when Jane inquires if the cow was milked again last night? "Yes," says Dan, and "I only wish I could find out who does it; it would not be well for him, I can tell you. This is the tenth time this fortnight that she has been milked. Oh! if it was not for this rheumatism in my hip, I would stay up some night and catch the thief in the act, have him arrested, and—"

"And then," remarks Esther, with an eye to the financial part of the milk question, "we should have just two quarts more to sell every day; that would be—let me see how much it would come to."

"Never mind," remarks John Teed, "how much it would come to, just hand me that dish of potatoes, please. They are so well mashed that I must eat some more. I can't bear potatoes with lumps all through them, can you Jane."

"No, John, I cannot," replies Jane.

"Neither can I," joins in William Cox; "if I ever marry I hope my wife will be as good a cook as Olive; if she prove so I shall be satisfied."

"Gim me 'nother piece of meat, do you hear," is the exclamation which comes from master Willie.

"Ask as a good boy should," remarks Dan, "and you shall have it."

"Gim me 'nother piece of meat, do you hear," says the young rascal a second time, louder than before.

A good sound box on the ear from his father, prevents further remarks coming from the unruly boy during the rest of the meal. However, after a slight pause, Dan gives him a piece of beef-steak, his mother in the meantime says:

"I wonder how that boy learns to be so rude."

"Why," replies John Teed, "by playing with those bad boys down near the carriage factory. I saw him there about nine o'clock this morning, and what's more, I can tell you that unless he keeps away from them he will be ruined."

"I'm going to take him in hand as soon as he gets a little older and make him toe the mark," says Dan. "Well Mudge,"—Dan nearly always calls his wife Mudge, for a pet name—"give me another cup of tea, woman, and then I'll go back to the factory, that is as soon as I have taken a pull or two at my pipe."

"What! are you going without eating some of the bread pudding I went to the trouble of making because I thought you would like it?" asks Olive.

"Oh, you've got pudding have you; all right, I'll have some if it's cold," replies Dan.

"Oh, yes, it's cold enough by this time. Come, Esther, help me to clear away these dishes, and you, Jane, please bring in the pudding, it is out on the door-step near the rain-water barrel."

The dishes having been cleared away, and the pudding brought, all ate a due share, and after some further conversation about the midnight milker of the cow, Esther remarks that she believes the thief to be one of the Micmac Indians from the camp up the road. Everybody laughs at such a wild idea, and they all leave the table. Esther, takes George from his chair, after first untying his feet, and then helps Olive to remove the dishes to the kitchen, where she washes them, and then goes to the sofa in the parlor to take a nap. Dan in the meantime has enjoyed his smoke and gone back to the factory, as has also William Cox. John Teed has gone up the Main Street to see his sister Maggie, and Jane has returned to Mr. Dunlap's. Willie is out in the street again with the bad boys, and Olive has just commenced to make a new plaid dress for George, who has gone to sleep in his little crib in the small sewing-room.

Esther, after sleeping for about an hour, comes into the dining room where Olive is sewing and says, "Olive, I am going out to take a walk, and if Bob should come while I am out, don't forget to tell him that I will be in this evening, and shall expect him."

"All right Esther," says her sister, "but you had better be careful about Bob, and how you keep company with him; you know what we heard about him only the day before yesterday."

"Oh, I don't believe a word of it," replied Esther. She looked at her sister for a moment, and then said in an injured tone, "I guess I am old enough to take care of myself. What! half-past two already? I must be off;" and off she went.

Supper being over, Esther put on her brown dress and took her accustomed seat on the front door step to talk to Dan, as he smoked his evening pipe. Jane dressed in her favorite white dress, trimmed with black velvet, her beautiful hair fastened in a true Grecian coil, and perfectly smooth at the temples, is in the parlor attending to her choice plants, presently her beau comes to spend the evening with her.

So the evening passes away. Olive has sung little George to sleep, carried him up to bed and retired herself. Dan has smoked his pipe and retired also. It was now ten o'clock. Esther still sat on the front step humming the tune of a well known Wesleyan hymn to herself as she gazed up at the stars, for it must be remembered that although she was not by any means pious, still, like a dutiful girl, she went to church with Dan and Olive. As the girl was just passing into womanhood, and felt that she must love something, it was perfectly natural for her to sit there and wait for Bob to make his appearance. About half-past ten Jane's beau took his departure, and Jane not having anything further to keep her up, decided to retire, and advised Esther to follow her example.

Esther took a last look up and down the street, and then went into the house with much reluctance. After locking the front door the girls went into the dining room and Jane lighted the lamp. Esther had taken off her shoes and thrown them on the floor, as was her custom, when it suddenly occurred to her that there was butter-milk in the cellar, and the same instant she made up her mind to have some. Taking the lamp from Jane, she runs into the cellar in her stocking feet, drinks about a pint of butter-milk and runs up again, telling her sister, who has been meanwhile in the dark dining room, that a large rat passed between her feet while in the cellar.

"Come right up to bed you silly girl," said Jane, "and don't be talking about rats at this time of night." So Jane took the lamp and Esther picked up her shoes, and they went to their bed-room.

After closing the door of their room, "Esther," said Jane, "you are foolish to think anything at all about Bob."

"Oh, mind your own business, Jane," Esther replied "let's say our prayers and retire;" and so they did.

CHAPTER II

THE FATAL RIDE

Esther and Jane arose on the morning of August 28th, 1878, as was their usual custom, at half-past six, and ate breakfast with the rest of the family.

After breakfast Jane went to Mrs. Dunlap's, Dan to his shoe factory with his brother-in-law, William Cox, John Teed also went to **his** work, and none of the family remained in the house but Olive and Esther, who commenced to wash up the breakfast dishes and put the dining room in order, so that part of their work at least should be finished before the two little boys came down stairs to have their childish wants attended to. What with making the beds and sweeping the rooms, and washing out some clothing for the boys, both Esther and Olive found plenty to occupy their time until the hour for preparing dinner arrived. When Olive commenced that rather monotonous operation, assisted by Esther, who, as she sat on the door-step between the dining room and kitchen paring potatoes, and placing them in a can of cold water beside her, attracted her sister's attention by her continued silence and the troubled expression of her countenance.

"What in the name of the sun ails you to-day, Esther?" inquired Olive, really worried by her little sister's sad appearance.

"Oh, nothing, Olive! only I was thinking that if—that if—that if—"

"Well! well, go on, go on, it is not necessary to say that if—five or six times in succession, is it, before telling me what's the matter with you, you nonsensical, giddy, hard-headed girl. I believe you have fallen in love so with Bob McNeal, that you are worrying yourself to death because you know he is too poor to marry you and you are afraid some rich girl will fall in love with him, and that he will marry her and give you the cold shoulder.

There, that's just what I think **is** the matter with you, and I can tell you one thing my young lady, and that is, that the sooner you get over your infatuation for that young man, the better for you, and the better for us all. There now, I'm done. No I'm not either, listen to me, girl, and don't make me angry by turning up your nose while I am giving you good advice."

"I'm not turning up my nose at you, Olive. I only felt like sneezing, and wanted to stop it before it had fully commenced, and how could I try to stop it except by working my nose in that way, when I have a big wet potato in one hand and this ugly old knife in the other, and all wet, too."

"Oh, nonsense, girl, don't keep on talking about ugly old knives and wet potatoes, but listen to me. I feel it in my bones that trouble is in store for us, and all through Bob McNeal. Now do be a good girl, and take my advice and never invite him to call again; because I tell you, Esther, that trouble is coming to you through that young man, for I feel it in my bones."

"Well, Olive, I will tell you the truth; the fact is that—why here's Jane! Why, Jane, what has brought you home at this time of day? It is only eleven, and dinner won't be ready for an hour."

Jane, who had just taken off her hat and hung it up in the hall, replied, "that as there was nothing more to be done at Dunlap's until the afternoon, she thought she might as well be at home attending to her plants as at the shop."

After looking at Esther and Olive a moment, she said, "What were you two putting your heads together about when I came in? Esther stopped talking as soon as she saw me, and Olive, I noticed that you went to the stove and poured so much water into the tea-kettle from the bucket that it ran over, just because you were looking at me instead of at the kettle. You are both up to something, I know you are. Now come, tell me all about it; is it a great secret? I won't tell anybody; tell me, do."

Esther, who has just finished paring the potatoes and is now putting them on the stove to boil, takes a seat in the dining room on the settee and has one of her sulky moods, during which she always declines to speak when spoken to.

Jane looks at her a second and then says in a playful manner, "Oh, it's all right, Esther, I can guess what it was; what nonsense. I'll go and attend to my plants. Why, I declare it's a quarter past eleven already, and I have got to comb my hair before dinner, too. Oh! my, how time flies!"

So off Jane goes to her plants in the parlor, leaving Esther in the dining room and Olive in the kitchen getting dinner ready as fast as she can.

Olive had just gone behind the kitchen door that leads into the yard to get another stick of wood for the fire when she was startled by a scream; she feels instinctively that one of her children is in danger, and she is right, for little George has just been saved from a horrible death by Maud Weldon, their next door neighbor. The little scamp had managed to crawl through the fence and get as far as the middle of the street, when Maud saw him, and was just in time to prevent him from being run over by a heavy wagon drawn by a pair of horses that were being driven at a breakneck pace past the house. Of course the fair Maud screamed, young women generally do at such times; but she saved George all the same. Her piercing shriek brought the stately Miss Sibley and her mother to the door of their house, which is almost directly opposite Dan's, and also caused Mrs. Mitchell and Mrs. Bell to become so nervous that they kept their children in the house for the rest of the day, when they heard of the dangerous adventure George had had, for they both arrived too late to witness the rescue. The watchfulness and care they both bestowed on their little ones for the next week was so much time thrown away, however, for it so happened that no more fast teams came through that particular street for about a month.

Well, after the brave blonde, Maud Weldon, had become the heroine of the hour, she went into Dan's cottage with Esther and Jane, who both ran out when they heard the scream. Olive had already taken her boy in, washed his little hands and face, put on his clean over-dress, and was now holding him in her lap in the large rocking-chair. Maud Weldon was in the parlor with Jane and Esther looking at the flowers and telling them about her new beau, how handsome he was, and that she intended to marry him if he asked her, winding up her conversation on the subject of beaux with the remark that she was bound not to die an old maid, but was going to get married for she wanted to have a house of her own to keep. And so the conversation ran on between the three girls in the parlor until dinner was nearly ready, when Mrs. Hicks, Maud's aunt, called her and she went home.

After dinner, Esther and Olive were washing the dishes in the kitchen and talking over George's narrow escape, when Esther suddenly made up her mind to tell her sister what she was about to do when Jane's rather unexpected return from the shop put an end to their conversation. So after having put all the dishes away in the pantry, she told Olive if she would promise not to tell anybody, not even Dan, she would tell her something that must be kept a secret, because if it became known it might make people nervous and could do no good.

"Very well," replied Olive, "wait until I get my sewing, then we will go into the parlor, you can tell me all about it, and I promise that I won't tell."

So they went into the parlor. Esther sat in the rocking-chair and Olive on the sofa.

"Well, Olive," said Esther. "Now don't laugh, for it is about a dream."

"A dream!" exclaimed Olive. "A dream! go on, let me hear it."

"Well," began Esther, "last night I sat for two hours on the front step looking at the stars. After I came in I went down into the cellar in my stocking feet and drank about a pint of butter-milk and a large rat ran between my feet; then Jane and I went to our room, shut the door, said our prayers and went to bed, and in a short time we both fell asleep, and I dreamt that when I got up in the morning every thing and every body was changed except myself. This cottage instead of being yellow was green; you, Dan, Jane, brother William, John Teed, Willie and George, all had heads like bears, and you all growled at me, but yet could talk, and, what was very strange, you all had eyes as large as horses' eyes, only they were as red as blood. While I was talking to you I heard a noise in the street and on going to the door I saw hundreds of black bulls with blue eyes, very bright blue eyes, coming towards the house, blood was dripping from their mouths and their feet made fire come out of the ground. On they came, roaring very loudly all the time, right straight for the house. They broke down the fence, I shut the front door, locked it and then ran to the back door and fastened it. Then they all commenced to butt the house so violently that it nearly fell over. It shook so that I woke up and found that I had fallen out of bed without waking Jane. So I got in again and soon fell asleep; but the dream is still in my mind. I can see it still, and wonder what it means until I get the head-ache. What do you think about it Olive? Do you think there is any truth in dreams? Did you ever know of one to come true, or do you think it was all caused by the pint of butter-milk and my going into the cellar in my stocking feet, and the rat?"

“Well,” said Olive, “I never could make up my mind fully on that subject; but of this I am certain, whatever Dan dreams comes true; there is no doubt about that. But don’t tell him anything about this dream, Esther, or he will be floundering around all night trying to find out what it means; or Jane either, because, perhaps, it will scare her so that she will be unable to sleep.”

“Don’t believe it, Olive, I have told Jane, and she says it was all caused by the butter-milk I drank. She says it made me see a rat in the cellar just after I had drank it, and that it was no wonder I saw bears and bulls, too, after I went to sleep. Oh, my sakes alive, if I only had a dream book, like the one Mrs. Emery used to have, I’d soon find out what it means. Do you know, Olive, I have a great mind to go out to the Indian camp this very afternoon and try if that fortune-telling squaw who told Maggie Teed’s fortune, and Mary Miller’s, too, can’t tell me all about it. I want to know if it means that something terrible is about to happen or not.”

“Well,” said Olive, “Esther, don’t talk any more about it but read your Bible, go to church, say your prayers, and ask God to take care of you; then you need never fear dreams or anything else, for you must always remember that God has more power than the devil, and always will have.”

“Oh!” replied Esther, with a smile, “it is all very Well for you to talk in that way, but I shouldn’t wonder if the devil saw more of me than he ever has yet before I die.”

“Oh, Esther, how can you talk so; you ought to be ashamed of yourself, and to think that you were brought up by grandmother too.”

And so the afternoon passed slowly away, the beautiful blue sky which had been so clear all day began to assume a darkish aspect, and threatening clouds spread themselves between the earth and heaven. By the time Dan and the rest had come home to supper, it looked very much like rain. Dan said it was going to rain sometime during the night; he knew it, because his rheumatism was bad.

Supper being ready, they all sat down and enjoyed it. After supper Dan took a smoke, Jane went to her accustomed seat in the parlor near her plants, William Cox and John Teed went out to see their girls, Olive put the boys to bed, and Esther sat down on the front door-step all by herself and sang “The Sweet By-and-bye” in a low voice.

The hands of the old fashioned clock in the dining room indicated ten minutes to eight, when a carriage drove up to the gate, and a well built young man jumped out, opened the gate and came in. As he entered the house he shook hands with Esther, saying as he did so: "Go and put on your hat and sack and take a ride with me Esther, and I will tell you why I did not call last evening as I promised." This young man was Bob McNeal, by trade a shoemaker, and a fine looking young fellow he was, too. His hair and eyes were black, features, rather handsome, and he wore a small black moustache.

As soon as Esther had received his invitation she ran up stairs, got her hat and sack, ran down again, jumped into the carriage, which was a buggy with room for two only, and off they drove. Jane came out to the front door and called after them, just as they were driving away: "You had better put the top up Bob, for it will certainly rain before long."

Dan, who had been sitting in the dining room in one of the easy chairs, remarked to Jane as he was going up stairs: "What a pity Bob McNeal is such a wild fellow. I'm afraid he will never amount to much. He is a remarkably fine workman too; he has improved in his work since I took him into the factory with me. Oh well, I suppose it's all right; good night Jane."

"Good night Dan," said Jane.

"I hope your rheumatism will be better in the morning."

"So do I," replied Dan. And up he went to bed, Jane returning to the parlor to wait for her beau.

Bob and Esther drove through Amherst, and turned down the road leading to the Marsh. They were going to take a ride into the country. Bob said that was the best road to take, and Esther did not care much which way they went, so she got a ride.

While driving through a small wood, Bob seemed to be suddenly seized with an attack of what lawyers are pleased to term emotional insanity, for he dropped the reins and leaped from the buggy. Upon reaching the ground, he drew from the side pocket of his coat a large revolver, and, pointing it at Esther, told her, in a loud voice, to get out of the buggy or he would kill her where she sat. She, of course, refused to do as he requested or rather commanded, and, as it was raining and becoming quite dark, she told him to get into the buggy and drive her home, and not act like a crazy man. The remark about acting like a crazy man seemed to enrage him past endurance, for he uttered several terrible oaths, and, aiming the revolver at her heart, was about to fire, when the sound of wheels were heard rumbling in the distance. He immediately jumped into the buggy, seized the reins, and drove at a breakneck pace through the pouring rain to Dan's cottage. Esther was wet through by the time they had arrived at the gate. She jumped out, opened the gate, entered the cottage and ran up stairs without noticing Jane, whom she passed in the hall. Bob, as soon as she got out, drove rapidly down the street.

As the hour was now ten o'clock, Esther immediately retired and, after crying herself to sleep, slept until morning. Jane entered the room about half an hour after her sister, engaged in prayer and then retired, without disturbing her.

For the next four days Esther seemed to be suffering from some secret sorrow. She could not remain in the house, but was continually on the street, or at some of the neighbors' houses, and every night she cried herself to sleep.

Of course her woe-begone appearance was noticed by the family, but they refrained from questioning her, for the simple reason that they supposed she and Bob had quarrelled; and as they did not approve of the attachment between him and Esther, they were rather glad that his visits had ceased, and gave no further attention to the matter, supposing that she would be herself again in a week or two. Bob's continued absence from the cottage—for he used to be there every other day—strengthened them in the belief that they were right in their supposition, and so they let the matter rest.

CHAPTER III

THE HAUNTED HOUSE

Supper is just over. Dan and Olive are in the parlor. Jane is up stairs in her room, talking to Esther who has retired early; it being only seven o'clock, she asks Esther: "How long she is going to continue to worry herself about Bob?"

Not receiving a reply, she puts on her heavy sack and remarks: "I am going over to see Miss Porter, and will soon return; it is so damp and foggy to-night that, I declare, it makes me feel sleepy too. I think I will follow your example, and retire early. Good night, I suppose you will be asleep by the time I get back;" and off she goes.

As the night is so very damp and disagreeable, all begin to feel sleepy long before half-past eight, and go up to their rooms.

Before Dan goes up stairs, he takes the bucket and brings some fresh water from the pump—which he, as usual, places on the kitchen table—taking a large tin dipper about half full up to his room for the children to drink during the night.

It is now about fifteen minutes to nine. Jane has just returned from her visit, and has gone to her room, which is in the front of the house, near the stairway, and directly next to Dan and Olive's room. She finds Esther crying, as usual, for the girl has actually cried herself to sleep every night since the fatal ride. After getting into bed, she says: "Oh, my, I forgot to put the lamp out," rises immediately and extinguishes the light, remarks to Esther that "it is very dark," bumps her head against the bed post, and finally settles herself down for a good sleep.

Esther, who has just stopped crying, remarks to Jane that "this is a wretched night," and says, "somehow I can't get to sleep."

"No wonder," says Jane, "you went to bed too early."

"Jane, this is September the fourth, aint it?" asks Esther.

"Yes," replies Jane. "Go to sleep and let me alone, I don't want to talk to you, I want to go to sleep. What if it is September the fourth."

"Oh nothing," replies Esther, "only it is just a week to-night, since I went riding with Bob! Oh, what will become of me?" and she instantly burst into another crying spell.

"Esther" said Jane, "Do you know I think you are losing your mind, and that if you keep on this way you will get so crazy that we will have to put you in the Insane Asylum." This had the desired effect, for she stopped instantly. For a few minutes everything was perfectly still. No sound was to be heard except the breathing of the two young girls, as they lay side by side in bed.

They had remained perfectly quiet, for about ten or fifteen minutes, when Esther jumped out of bed with a scream, exclaiming that there was a mouse under the bed clothes.

Her scream startled her sister, who was almost asleep, and she also got out of bed and lit the lamp, for she is as much afraid of mice as Esther is. They both searched the bed, but could not find the supposed mouse, supposing it to be inside the mattrass. Jane exclaimed "Oh pshaw, what fools we are to be sure to be scared at a little harmless mouse; if there really is one here it can do us no harm, for see, it is inside the mattrass, look how the straw is being moved about. The mouse has gotten inside and can't get out, because there is no hole in the ticking. Let us go back to bed Esther. It can do us no harm now." So they put out the light, and got into bed again. After listening for a few minutes without hearing the straw move in the mattrass, they both fell asleep.

On the following night the girls heard something moving under their bed. Esther exclaimed: "There is that mouse again, Jane. Let us get up and kill it. I'm not going to be worried by mice every night."

So they both arose, and on hearing a rustling in a green paste-board box, filled with patch-work, which was under the bed, they placed it out in the middle of the room and were much amazed to see the box jump up in the air about a foot and then fall over on its side. The girls could not believe their own eyes; so Jane placed the box in its old position in the middle of the room, and both watched it intently, when to their amazement the same thing occurred again. The girls were now really frightened, and screamed as loudly as they could for Dan, who put on some clothing and came into their room to ascertain what was the matter. They told him what had just taken place, but he only laughed, and after pushing the box under the bed, and remarking that they must be insane or perhaps had been dreaming, he went back to bed grumbling because his rest had been disturbed.

The next morning the girls both declared that the box had really moved; but, as nobody believed them, they saw it was of no use to talk of the matter. Jane went to the shop, Dan to his shoe factory, and William Cox and John Teed about their business as usual, leaving Olive and Esther to attend to their household duties. After dinner Olive took her sewing into the parlor, and Esther went out to walk. The afternoon was delightful, and there was quite a breeze blowing from the bay. Walking is very pleasant when there is no dust; but Amherst is such a dusty little village, especially when the wind blows from the bay, that it is impossible to walk on any of the streets with comfort on a windy day during the summer. Esther found this to be the case, so she retraced her steps homeward, stopping at the post office and at Bird's book store, where she bought a bottle of ink from Miss Blanche. On arriving at the cottage she hung up her hat and joined Olive in the parlor, took little George on her lap, and, after singing him to sleep, lay down on the sofa and took a nap.

After supper Esther took her accustomed seat on the door-step, remaining there until the moon had risen. It was a beautiful moonlight night, almost as bright as day. While seated there gazing at the moon, she said to herself, "Well there is one thing certain anyhow, I am going to have good luck all this month, for on Sunday night I saw the new moon over my shoulder."

At half-past eight o'clock, Esther complained of feeling feverish and was advised by Olive and Jane to go to bed, which she did.

About ten o'clock Jane retired for the night. After she had been in bed some fifteen minutes, Esther jumped with a sudden bound into the centre of the room, taking all the bed clothes with her.

"My God!" she exclaimed, "what can be the matter with me! Wake up Jane, wake up! I'm dying, I'm dying!" "Dying!" responded Jane; "why dying people don't speak in that loud tone. Wait until I light the lamp, don't die in the dark Esther."

Jane thought her sister only had the night mare, but when she lit the lamp, she was considerably alarmed by her sister's appearance. There stood Esther in the centre of the room, her short hair almost standing on end, her face as red as blood, and her eyes really looked as if they were about to start from their sockets, her hands were grasping the back of a chair so tightly that her nails sank into the soft wood. She was truly an object to look on with amazement, as she stood there in her white night gown trembling with fear. Her sister called as loudly as she could for assistance; for Jane, too, was pretty well frightened by this time, and did not know what to do. Olive was the first to enter the room, having first thrown a shawl around her shoulders, for the night was very chilly. Dan, put on his coat and pants in a hurry, as did also William Cox, and John Teed, and the three men entered the room about the same time.

"Why what in the name of thunder ails you Esther?" asked Dan. William and John exclaimed in the same breath, "She's mad!"

Olive was speechless with amazement, while they stood looking at the girl, not knowing what to do to relieve her terrible agony. She became very pale and seemed to be growing weak; in fact, she became so weak in a short time that she had to be assisted to the bed. After sitting on the edge of the bed for a moment, and gazing about the room with a vacant stare, she started to her feet with a wild yell, and said she felt like bursting into pieces.

"Great Heavens," exclaimed Olive, "What shall we do with her; she is crazy?"

Jane, who always retains her presence of mind, took her sister's hand and said in a soothing tone: "Come Esther, get into bed again." As they found that she could not do so without assistance, Olive and Jane helped her, and placed the bed clothing over her again. As soon as she had been assisted to bed she said in a low choking voice, "I am swelling up and shall certainly burst, I know I shall."

Dan looked at her face and remarked in a startled tone. "Why, the girl is swelling, Olive, just look at her, look at her hands too, see how swollen they are, and she is as hot as fire."

She was literally burning up with fever, and yet as pale as death, while only a few minutes before her face was as red as blood, and her entire person as cold as ice. What a strange case, pale when hot, and blood red when cold, yet such was really the fact.

While the family stood looking at her, wondering what would relieve her, for her entire body had swollen to an enormous size and she was screaming with pain and grinding her teeth as if in a fit, a loud report like thunder was heard in the room. They all started to their feet instantly and seemed paralyzed with fear.

"My God!" exclaimed Olive, "the house has been struck by lightning and I know my poor boys are killed?"

After giving vent to this exclamation, she rushed from the room to her own where the children were, and found them both sleeping soundly, so she returned to the room where they all stood looking at Esther, and wondering what had produced the terrible sound. On entering, Olive told them that the boys were both sound asleep.

"I wonder what that awful noise was?" she said. Going to the window and raising the curtain she saw that the stars were shining brightly and was then satisfied that it had not been thunder they had heard. Just as she let the curtain drop, three terrific reports were heard, apparently directly under the bed. They were so loud that the whole room shook, and Esther who a moment before had been swollen to such an enormous size, immediately assumed her natural appearance, and sank into a state of calm repose. As soon as they found that it was sleep and not death that had taken possession of her, they all left the room except Jane, who went back to bed beside her sister, but could not sleep a wink for the balance of the night.

The next day Esther remained in bed until about nine o'clock, when she arose, seemingly all right again, and got her own breakfast. As her appetite was not as good as usual, all she could eat was a small piece of bread and butter and a large green pickle, washed down with a cup of strong tea. She helped Olive with her work as usual, and after dinner took a walk past the post office, around the block and back to the cottage again. At supper the usual conversation about the strange sounds took place, all wondering what had caused them. As no one could ascertain the cause they gave it up as something too strange to think about, and all agreed not to let the neighbors know anything about it, because they argued, that, as no one would be likely to believe that such strange sounds had been heard under the bed, the best thing to do was to keep the matter quiet.

About four nights after the loud reports had been heard, Esther had another similar attack. It came on about ten o'clock at night, just as she was getting in bed. This time, however, she managed to get into bed before the attack had swelled her up to any great extent. Jane, who had already retired, advised her to remain perfectly still, and perhaps the attack would pass off, but how sadly was she mistaken. Esther had only been in bed about five minutes when, to the amazement of the girls, all the bed clothing flew off and settled down in the far corner of the room. They could see them going for the lamp was burning dimly on the table. They both screamed, and then Jane fainted dead away. The family rushed into the room as before, and were so frightened that they did not know what to do. There lay the bed clothes in the corner, Esther all swollen up, Jane in a dead faint, and perhaps really dead for all they knew, for by the glare of the lamp, which Dan held in his hand, she looked more dead than alive. Olive was the first to come to her senses. Taking up the bed clothes, she placed them over her sisters. Just as she had done so, off they flew again to the same corner of the room. In less time than it takes to count three, the pillow flew from under Esther's head and struck John Teed in the face. He immediately left the room, saying that he had had enough. He could not be induced to return and sit on the edge of the bed with the others, who in that way managed to keep the clothes in their place. Jane had by this time recovered from her swoon. William Cox went down to the kitchen for a bucket of water to bathe the Esther's head, which was aching terribly. Just as he got to the door of the room again with the bucket of water, a succession of reports were heard, which seemed to come from the bed where Esther lay. They were so very loud that the whole room shook, and Esther, who had a moment before been swollen up, commenced to assume her natural appearance, and in a few minutes fell into a pleasant sleep. As everything seemed now to be all right again, everybody went back to bed.

In the morning Esther and Jane were both very weak, particularly Esther. She, however, got up when her sister did, and lay down on the sofa in the parlor. At breakfast they all agreed that a doctor had better be called in. So in the afternoon Dan left the factory early and went to see Dr. Caritte. The doctor laughed when Dan told him what had occurred. He said he would call in the evening and remain until one in the morning if necessary, but did not hesitate to say that what Dan had told him was all nonsense, remarking that he knew no such tomfoolery would occur while he was in the house.

As the hands of the clock pointed to ten, in walked the doctor. Bidding everybody a hearty good evening, he took a seat near Esther, who had been in bed since nine o'clock, but as yet had not been afflicted with one of her strange attacks. The doctor felt her pulse, looked at her tongue, and then told the family that she seemed to be suffering from nervous excitement and had evidently received a tremendous shock of some kind. Just as he had said these words, the pillow from under her head left the bed, with the exception of one corner, which remained under her head, straightened itself out as if filled with air, and then went back to its place again. The doctor's large, blue eyes opened to their utmost capacity, as he asked in a low tone: "Did you all see that; it went back again."

"So it did," remarked John Teed, "but if it moves out again it will not go back, for I intend to hold on to it, even if it did bang me over the head last night."

John had no sooner spoken these words than out came the pillow from under Esther's head as before. He waited until it had just started back again, and then grasped it with both hands, and held on with all his strength. The pillow, however, was pulled from him by some invisible power stronger than himself. As he felt it being pulled away, his hair actually stood on end.

"How wonderful!" exclaimed Dr. Caritte.

Just as the doctor arose from his chair, the reports under the bed commenced, as on the previous night. The doctor looked beneath the bed, but failed to ascertain what caused the sounds. When he walked to the door the sounds followed him, being now produced on the floor of the room. In about a minute after this, off went the bed clothes again, and before they had been put back on the bed, the sound as of some person writing on the wall with a sharp instrument was heard. All looked at the wall whence the sound of writing came, when to their great astonishment there was seen written, near the head of the bed, in large characters, these words: "Esther Cox, you are mine to kill." Everybody could see the writing plainly, and yet only a moment before nothing was to be seen but the blank wall.

The reader can imagine their utter amazement at what had just taken place. There they stood around the bed of this wonderful girl, each watching the other to see that there was no deception. They knew these marvellous things had taken place, for all heard them with their own ears and beheld them with their own eyes. Still, they could not believe their own senses, it was all so strange. But the writing on the wall—what did it mean, and how came it there? God only knew.

As Doctor Caritte stood in the doorway for a moment wondering to himself what it all meant, a large piece of plaster came flying from the wall of the room, having in its flight turned a corner and fallen at his feet. The good doctor picked it up mechanically and placed it on a chair. He was too astonished to speak. Just as he did so, the poundings commenced again with redoubled power, this time shaking the entire room. It must be remembered that during all this time Esther lay upon the bed, almost frightened to death by what was occurring. After this state of things had continued for about two hours, everything became quiet and she went to sleep. The doctor said he would not give her any medicine until the next morning, when he would call at nine and give her something to quiet her nerves; for she was certainly suffering from some nervous trouble. As to the sounds and movements of objects, he could not account for them, but thought if she became strong again they would cease.

In the morning the doctor called as he had promised, and was much surprised to see Esther up and dressed, helping Olive to wash the dishes. She told him that she felt all right again, only she was so nervous that any sudden noise made her jump. Having occasion to go down into the cellar with a pan of milk, she came running up, out of breath, exclaiming that there was some one down in the cellar, for a piece of plank had been thrown at her. The doctor went down to see for himself, Esther remaining in the dining room; for it must be borne in mind that the cellar door opens into the dining room. In a moment he came up again remarking that there was nobody down there to throw a piece of plank, nor anything else.

"Esther, come down with me," said he. So down they both went, when, to their great surprise, several potatoes came flying at their heads. That was enough. They both beat a hasty retreat. The doctor left the house, and called again in the evening, with several very powerful sedatives, morphia being one, which he administered to Esther about ten o'clock as she lay in bed. She still complained of her nervousness, and said she felt as if electricity was passing all through her body. He had given her the medicine, and had just remarked that she would have a good night's rest when the loud sounds commenced, only they were much louder and in more rapid succession than on the previous nights. Presently the sounds left the room and were heard on the roof of the house. The doctor instantly left the house and went out into the street, hearing the sounds while in the open air. He returned to the house more nonplussed than ever, and told the family that from the street it seemed as if some person was on the roof with a heavy sledge hammer pounding away to try and break through the shingles. Being a moonlight night he could see distinctly that there was not any one out on the roof. He remained until twelve. Everything becoming quiet again, he then departed, saying he would call the next day. When he had got as far as the gate, the sounds on the roof commenced again with great violence, and continued until he had gone about two hundred yards from the cottage, at which distance he could still hear them distinctly.

The next week it became known throughout Amherst that strange things were going on at Dan Teed's cottage. The mysterious sounds had been heard by people in the street as they passed the house, and the poundings now commenced in the morning and were to be heard all day long. Esther always felt relieved when the sounds were produced by the unknown power.

Dr. Caritte called every night, and sometimes during the day, but could not afford her the slightest relief. One night, about three weeks after the doctor's first visit, as he and the family were standing around her bed listening to the loud knockings, Esther suddenly threw her arms up towards the head of the bed, and seemed to be seized with a spasm, for she became cold and perfectly rigid. While in this state she commenced to talk, and told all that had occurred between herself and Bob McNeal on the night of the fatal ride. This was the first anybody knew of the affair, for she had never told of it, and Bob had never been seen in the locality after that night. When she came to her senses again, they told her what had been said by herself during the strange state from which she had just emerged. Upon hearing this she commenced to cry, and told them that it was all true; that he had threatened her with his revolver, but becoming frightened by the sound of wheels in the distance, had driven her home without offering her any further show of violence.

"There!" exclaimed Olive, "Didn't I tell you that I felt it in my bones, that harm would come to you through that young man, and now you see he really is at the bottom of all this. Ah, it is Bob, who makes all these strange sounds about the house; I know he is the cause." Instantly three distinct reports were heard, shaking the whole house with their violence.

"Do you know doctor," said Jane, "that I believe that whatever agency makes these noises, it can hear and understand what we are talking about, and perhaps see us." The moment she had finished the sentence, three distinct reports were heard as loud as before.

"Ask if it can hear us doctor?" said Dan. "Can you, whatever you are, hear what we say?" asked Dr. Caritte.

Again three reports were heard, which shook the entire house.

"Why, that is very singular," remarked the doctor. "I believe Jane was right, it can hear."

"Well, let us try again," said Dan. "If you can see and hear, tell us how many persons are in this room?" Esther did not know how many were present, for she was lying in the bed, with her face buried in the pillow trembling with fear. As Dan did not receive an answer, he asked again.

"How many persons are in the room? Give us a knock on the floor for each one." Five distinct knocks were made by the strange force on the floor, and there were just five persons in the room, as follows:—Dr. Caritte, Dan, Olive, Esther and Jane, William Cox and John Teed having left the room after Esther had burried her face in the pillow. "Well, it certainly is strange remarked the doctor, but I must go, it is getting late." So he departed after saying he would call the next evening.

The next evening the Doctor called and remained for about an hour, but as nothing occurred he departed feeling rather disappointed. For the next three weeks no one could tell when the manifestations would take place. Sometimes they would commence in the morning and continue all day, and at other times they would only take place after Esther had retired. It had now become a settled fact that Esther must be in the house or there would be no manifestations of any kind. They never occurred during her absence.

About one month after the commencement of the manifestations, Dr. Edwin Clay, the well known Baptist clergyman, called at the house to behold the wonders with his own eyes. He had read some little account of them in the newspapers, but was desirious of seeing and hearing for himself, not taking much stock, as the saying is, in what other people told him about the affair. However, he was fortunate enough to have his desire fully gratified. He heard the loudest kind of knocks, in answer to his various questions, saw the mysterious writing on the wall, and left the house fully satisfied that Esther did not produce any of the manifestations herself, and that the family did not assist her as some people believed. He, however, was of the opinion that through the shock her system had received the night she went riding, she had become in some mysterious manner an electric battery. His theory being, that invisible flashes of lightening left her person, and that the knocks which every body could hear distinctly, were simply minute claps of thunder. He lectured on his theory, and drew large audiences as he always does, no matter what the subject is. Perfectly satisfied that the manifestations are genuine, he has nobly defended Esther Cox from the platform and the pulpit.

Rev. R.A. Temple, the well known Wesleyan minister pastor of the Wesleyan Church in Amherst, has witnessed some of the manifestations. He saw, among other strange things, a bucket of cold water become agitated, and to all appearances boil, while standing on the kitchen table.

As soon as people in the village found that such eminent men as Dr. Clay, Dr. Caritte and Rev. Dr. Temple took an interest in the case, it became quite fashionable for people in the village to call at Dan's little cottage to see Esther Cox and witness the wonderful manifestations. While the house was filled with visitors, large crowds often stood outside unable to gain admittance. On several occasions the village police force had to be called out to keep order, so anxious were people to see and hear for themselves.

Many believed and still believe the whole affair a fraud, and others say that Esther mesmerizes people, and they think they hear and see things which never have an existence. Dr. Nathan Tupper is of this belief, although he has never witnessed a single manifestation.

Dr. Caritte, who continued to be one of the daily callers at the cottage, would have a theory one day that would seem to account for the manifestations he had witnessed, and the next day something wonderful would occur and upset his latest theory completely, so that he finally gave up in despair and became simply a passive spectator. Things went on in this way until December, when Esther was taken ill with diphtheria, and confined to her bed for about two weeks, during which time the manifestations ceased entirely. After she had recovered from her illness, she went to Sackville, N.B., to visit her other married sister, Mrs. John Snowden, remaining at her house for about two weeks. While there she was entirely free from the manifestations.

On returning to Dan's cottage the most startling part of the case was developed. One night while in bed with her sister Jane in another room, her room having been changed to see if that would put a stop to the affair, she told her sister that she could hear a voice saying to her that the house was to be set on fire that night by a ghost. The voice also said that it had once lived on the earth, but had been dead for some years. The members of the household were called in at once, and told what had been said. They only laughed and remarked that no such thing as that could take place, because there were no ghosts. Dr. Clay had said it was all electricity. "And," added Dan, "electricity can't set the house on fire unless it comes from a cloud in the form of lightning." As they were talking the matter over, to the amazement of all present, a lighted match fell from the ceiling to the bed, and would have set it on fire had not Jane put it out instantly. During the next ten minutes, eight or ten lighted matches fell on the bed and about the room, but were all extinguished before any harm could be done. In the course of the night the loud knockings commenced. The family could now all converse with the invisible power in this way. It would knock once for a negative answer, and three times for an answer in the affirmative, giving two knocks when in doubt about a reply. Dan asked if the house would be set on fire, and the reply was three loud knocks on the floor, meaning yes; and a fire was started about five minutes afterwards. The ghost took a dress belonging to Esther that was hanging on a nail in the wall near the door, rolled it up, and, before any of the persons in the room could remove it from under the bed, where the ghost had placed it before their very eyes, it was all in a blaze. It was extinguished, however, without being much injured by the fire. The next morning all was consternation in the cottage. Dan and Olive were afraid that the ghost would start a fire in some inaccessible place and burn the house down. They were both convinced that it really was a ghost, "for" said Olive, "nothing but the devil or a ghost with evil designs, could do so terrible a thing as start a fire in a cottage at the dead of night."

Dr. Clay's theory might be true, but it was not clear to them how electricity could go about a house gifted with the cunning of a fiend. "It is true," said Dan, "that lightning often sets fire to houses and barns, but it has never yet been known to roam about a man's house, as this strange power does. And as Esther can hear it speak, and it does whatever it says it will, why I believe it to be a ghost, or else the devil." While Olive was churning in the kitchen one morning about three days after the fire under the bed, she noticed smoke coming from the cellar. Esther was seated in the dining room when Olive first saw the smoke, and had been seated there for the last hour, previous to which she had been in the kitchen assisting her sister to wash the breakfast dishes as was her custom. On seeing the smoke, both she and Esther were for the moment utterly paralyzed with fear. What they so dreaded had at last come to pass. The house was evidently on fire, and that fire set by a devilish ghost. What was to be done? Olive was the first to recover from the shock. Seizing the bucket of drinking water, always kept standing on the kitchen table, she rushed down the cellar stairs, and was horrified at the sight which burst upon her view. There in the far corner of the cellar was a barrel of shavings blazing almost to the floor above. In the meantime Esther had reached the cellar, and stood looking at the crackling flames in blank astonishment. The water Olive had poured into the barrel was not enough to quench the flames, for in the excitement of the moment she had spilled more than half of it on her way down. What was to be done? The house would catch and probably be burned to the ground, and they would be rendered homeless.

"Oh! if Dan were at home, he could put it out," Olive managed to articulate, for both she and Esther were nearly suffocated with the dense black smoke with which the cellar was filled, and now the barrel itself had caught. The cellar was very small, and everything in it would soon be blazing unless the fire could be extinguished at once.

"Oh! what shall we do," cried Esther, "what shall we do?"

"Run out in the street and cry fire as loud as you can. Come, let's run at once or the whole house will burn down," exclaimed Olive, by this time wild with fear.

So, both she and Esther ran up stairs and out into the street, crying "fire! fire!" Of course their cries aroused the whole neighborhood. At the moment a gentleman, a stranger in the village, who happened to be passing, instantly threw off his coat, rushed into the cottage, picked up a mat from the dining room floor, and was down in the cellar in a second. He put the fire entirely out, and then, without waiting to be thanked, walked out of the cottage and was soon lost to view in the distance; and, what is remarkably strange, nobody knows who he was or whence he came, for from that day he has not been seen.

The news of the fire which the ghost had set in Dan's cellar soon travelled all over the country and created a great deal of curiosity. People who had set the whole affair down as a fraud began to think that perhaps it was all true after all, for certainly no young girl could set fire to a barrel of shavings in the cellar and be at that instant in another part of the house, under the watchful eye of an older sister, who was continually at her side. The fact that both the little boys were out in the front yard at the time the fire was kindled, and consequently could not have had anything to do with setting it, was also calculated to throw an air of mystery around the whole affair.

The family believed that it had been started by the ghost. The fire marshals of the village seemed to be of the opinion that Esther set both fires herself; the villagers held various opinions. Dr. Nathan Tupper, suggested that if a good raw hide whip were laid over her back by a strong arm, the manifestations would cease at once. Fortunately for Esther, no one had the right or power to beat her as if she were a slave, and so the mystery still remained unsolved.

For the next week manifestations continued to take place daily and were as powerful as ever. The excitement in Amherst was intense. If the cottage in which Dan lived should catch fire when the wind was blowing from the bay, the fire would spread, and if the wind was favorable for such a terrible calamity, the whole village would soon be reduced to ashes.

As if to pile horror upon horror, one night, as Esther and the entire family were seated in the parlor, the ghost appeared. Esther started to her feet and seemed for the moment paralyzed with terror. In a second or two, however, she recovered her self-possession, and pointing with a trembling hand to a distant corner of the room, exclaimed in a hoarse and broken voice:

"Look there! Look there! My **God**, it is the ghost! Don't you all see him? There he stands all in grey; see how his eyes are glaring at me and he laughs when he says I must leave the house to-night or he will start a fire in the loft under the roof and burn us all to death. Oh, what shall I do, where shall I go; the ground is covered with snow—and yet I cannot remain here, for he will do what he threatens; he always does."

"Oh, I wish I were dead." After this exclamation, she fell to the floor and burst into an agony of grief. "Well," said Dan, after lifting her up, "Something will have to be done, and quickly, too. The wind is blowing hard to-night, and if the ghost does as he threatens, the house will burn down sure, and perhaps the whole village. You must go, Esther. Remember, I don't turn you out; it is this devil of a ghost who drives you from your home."

They all knew none of the neighbors would shelter Esther, because they all feared the ghost. What was to be done? Heaven only knew. It suddenly occurred to Dan that John White would perhaps give her shelter, for he had always taken a deep interest in the manifestations, and had often expressed pity for the unhappy girl. So Dan, after putting on his heavy coat—for it was snowing fast, and the night was intensely cold—went to White's house. After knocking for some time, the door was opened by John White himself. He looked at Dan a moment in amazement, and then exclaimed in an inquiring tone:

"What's the matter, Teed? Has the house burned to the ground or has the girl burst all to pieces?"

Dan explained his mission in a few words. When he had finished, White thought a moment, and then said:

"Wait until I ask my wife; if she says yes, all right, you may bring her here to-night." He asked his wife, and fortunately for the miserable girl, she said "yes," and that very night Esther Cox changed her home.

CHAPTER IV

THE WALKING OF THE GHOST

When John White took Esther to his house to reside, he performed a charitable deed, which no man in the village but himself had the heart to do. Both he and his good wife showed, by the kindness with which they treated the poor unhappy girl, that Heaven had at least inspired two hearts with that greatest of all virtues—**Charity**.

It was now January, 1879,—just four months since the manifestations first commenced. Esther had been at White's residence for two weeks, and had not seen anything of the ghost. She had improved very much in that short time, her nervousness having almost subsided, and she was contented and happy. Mrs. White, who found her of great assistance in the house, had become much attached to the girl, and treated her with the same kindness that she did her own children.

Towards the end of the third week her old enemy—the ghost—returned.

While Esther was scrubbing the hall at her new home, she was astonished to see her scrubbing brush disappear from her hand. When the ghost told her that he had taken it, she became much alarmed and screamed for Mrs. White, who, with her daughter Mary, searched the hall for it in vain. After they had abandoned their search, to the great astonishment of all, the brush fell from the ceiling—just grazing Esther's head in its fall. Here was a new manifestation of the ghostly power. He was able to take a solid substance from this material world of ours, and render it invisible by taking it into his mysterious state of existence; and, if he could take one object why not another; if a brush, why not a broom? But why speculate on so great a mystery? The ghost did it, and as we must draw the line somewhere, it is better to draw it here than to allow our minds to become dazed by such fellows as ghosts. Many other remarkable manifestations continued to take place almost daily for the next two weeks. The ghost could now tell how much money people had in their pockets, both by knocking and by telling Esther. He would answer any question asked in the above mentioned manner, and behaved himself very well indeed until the end of the sixth week, when his true devilish nature broke out again. He commenced setting fires about the house, and walking so that he could be heard distinctly. Of course John White would not run the risk of having his house burned down. So he persuaded Esther to remain during the day in his dining saloon, which stands opposite the well known book store of G.G. Bird, on the principal street.

While standing behind the counter in the dining saloon, also while she worked in the adjoining kitchen, many new and wonderful things were witnessed by the inhabitants of Amherst and by strangers from a distance, and many plans were tried to prevent the manifestations. Among others, some one suggested that if she could stand on glass they would cease. So pieces of glass were put into her shoes, but as their presence caused her head to ache and her nose to bleed, without stopping the manifestations, the idea was abandoned.

One morning the door of the large stove in the kitchen adjoining the saloon was opened and shut by the ghost, much to the annoyance of Mr. White, who with an old axe handle so braced the door that it could not be moved by any known mundane power, unless the axe handle was first removed. A moment afterwards, however, the ghost, who seemed never to leave Esther's presence while she was in the saloon, lifted the door off its hinges, removed the axe handle from the position in which it had been placed, and, after throwing them some distance into the air, let both fall to the floor with a tremendous crash. Mr. White was speechless with astonishment, and immediately called in Mr. W.H. Rogers, Inspector of Fisheries for Nova Scotia. After bracing the door as before, the same wonderful manifestation was repeated, in the presence of Mr. Rogers. On another occasion, a clasp-knife belonging to little Fred, Mr. White's son, was taken from his hand by the ghost, who instantly stabbed Esther in the back with it, leaving the knife sticking in the wound, which bled profusely.

Fred, after drawing the knife from the wound, wiped it, closed it and put it in his pocket. The ghost took it from his pocket, and in a second stuck it in the same wound. Fred again obtained possession of the knife, and this time hid it so that it could not be found, even by a ghost.

There is something still more remarkable, however, about the following manifestation: Some person tried the experiment of placing three or four large iron spikes on Esther's lap while she was seated in the Dining Saloon. To the astonishment of everybody, the spikes were not removed by the ghost, but instead, became too hot to be handled with comfort, and a second afterwards were thrown by the ghost to the far end of the saloon, a distance of twenty feet.

During her stay at the saloon the ghost commenced to move the furniture about in the broad daylight. On one occasion a large box, weighing fifty pounds, moved was a distance of fifteen feet without the slightest visible cause. The very loud knocking commenced again and was heard by crowds of people, the saloon being continually filled with visitors. Among other well known inhabitants of Amherst who saw the wonders at this period, I may mention William Hillson, Daniel Morrison, Robt. Hutchinson, who is John White's son-in-law, and J. Albert Black, Esq., editor of the **Amherst Gazette**.

Towards the latter part of March, Esther went to Saint John, New Brunswick, and while there was the guest of Captain James Beck, and remained at his house for three weeks under the protection of his wife. Her case was investigated by a party of gentlemen, well known in Saint John as men whose minds have a scientific turn. Doctor Alward, Mr. Amos Fales, Mr. Alex. Christie, Mr. Ritchie, and many others witnessed the manifestations, and talked with the ghost by the aid of the knocks on the wall and furniture, and, strange to relate, other ghosts came and conversed also; among them one who said his name was Peter Cox, and another who gave the name of Maggie Fisher. All claimed to have lived on the earth before they entered the land of ghosts, but none were apparently as strong and healthy as the old original fire fiend of the cottage, who now gave the name of Bob Nickle, and said that when he lived on the earth he had been a shoemaker. The ghost who called himself Peter Cox, claimed to be a relation of Esther's, and said he had been in ghost land about forty years; he was a quiet old fellow, and did all he could to prevent Bob Nickle and Maggie Fisher from breaking the articles which they threw, and from using profane language, a habit in which **they** were fond of indulging.

Dr. Alward and his scientific friends also conversed with the ghosts by calling over the alphabet, the ghosts knocking at the correct letters, and in that way long communications were spelled out to the satisfaction of those present.

After remaining in Saint John about three weeks, Esther returned to Amherst, and accepted an invitation to visit Mr. and Mrs. Van Amburgh, who reside about three miles from the village. She remained eight weeks with them, during which period the ghosts allowed her to enjoy the calm repose of a life in the woods, the Van Amburgh farm being literally situated in the woods.

At the expiration of the eighth week she returned to Amherst, and went back to Dan's cottage to reside, being employed during the day in White's Dining Saloon. The manifestations soon commenced again, and were as powerful as when the author commenced his investigation of the case.

CHAPTER V

THE AUTHOR AND THE GHOSTS

I closed my engagement with the Dramatic Company of which I was a member, in Newfoundland, and went to Amherst, to expose, if possible, Esther Cox, the great Amherst Mystery.

Where occasion requires allusion to myself, I shall simply say the author.

At seven o'clock on the morning of June 21st, 1879, as the sun was shining brightly, and the cool breeze was blowing from the bay, the author entered the haunted house. After placing his umbrella in a corner of the dining room, and his satchel on the table, he seated himself in one of the easy chairs to await results. Esther and Olive were present. He had been in the room about five minutes when, to his great astonishment, his umbrella was thrown a distance of fifteen feet, going over his head in its flight. At the same instant a large carving knife came jumping over the girl's head, and fell near him. Not at all pleased with this kind of a reception on the part of the ghosts, he left the room and went into the parlor, taking his satchel with him, and there sat down paralyzed with wonder and astonishment. He had been seated only a moment when his satchel was thrown a distance of ten feet. At the same instant a large chair came flying across the room striking the one on which he was seated, nearly knocking it from under him. It suddenly occurred to him that he would take a walk, during which he could admire the beauties of the village.

On his return to the cottage, the ghosts commenced their deviltry again with redoubled violence. He had no sooner entered the house than all the chairs in the parlor—and there were seven by actual count—fell over. Concluding not to remain in that room, he went to the dining room, when the chairs in that, his favorite room in every house, went through the same performance. Feeling hungry, not yet having had his breakfast, he sat down to a good substantial meal, Esther sitting directly opposite. After pouring out his coffee, she handed it to him with the remark, "Oh, you will soon get used to them; I don't think they like you." "No," he replied, "I do not think they do either. In fact, I am satisfied they do not; but, having come here to investigate, I shall remain until they drive me from the house." While eating breakfast the ghosts commenced to hammer on the table. By the system in use by the family when conversing with them, he carried on a long conversation, they answering by knocks on the bottom of the table. Before entering into the conversation, however, he sat so that Esther's hands and feet were in full view. The ghosts told the number of his watch, also the dates of coins in his pocket, and beat correct time when he whistled the tune of "Yankee Doodle." Chairs continued to fall over until dinner, during which there was a slight cessation of manifestations.

After dinner, the author lay down upon the parlor sofa to take a nap, as is his custom in the afternoon. Esther came into the room for a newspaper. He watched her very closely, keeping one eye open and the one next her shut, so that she would think he was asleep. While watching her intently to see that she did not throw anything herself, a large glass paper weight, weighing fully a pound, came whizzing through the air from the far corner of the room, where it had been on a shelf, a distance of fully fifteen feet from the sofa. Fortunately for the author, instead of striking his head, which was evidently the intention of the ghost who threw it, it struck the arm of the sofa with great force, rebounding to a chair, upon which it remained after it had spun around for a second or two. Being very anxious to witness the manifestations, he requested Esther to remain in the room, which she did. After seating herself in the rocking chair, little George came into the room, when she placed the little fellow on her lap and sang to him. As the author lay there watching her, one of the child's copper-toed shoes was taken off by a ghost and thrown at him with great force, striking his head. The place struck was very sore for three or four days. The balance of the day passed quietly away. Evening came, and the author had a good night's rest in the haunted house of which he had heard so much. The next day being Sunday, everything was peaceful in the cottage, though why the ghosts should respect the Sabbath the author has never been able to ascertain; however they always remain quiet on that day. On Monday morning the ghosts commenced their mad pranks again, and seemed ready for anything. At breakfast, the lid of the stone-china sugar bowl disappeared from the table, and, in about ten minutes, fell from the ceiling. After breakfast; over went the table; then the chairs all fell over, and several large mats were pitched about the room. The author immediately left the room and went into the parlor, when, to his astonishment, a flower pot containing a large plant in full bloom was taken from its place in the bay window and set down in the middle of the room and a large tin can filled with water was brought from the kitchen and placed beside it. During the afternoon a large inkstand and two empty bottles were thrown at him. The ghosts also undressed little George, and, as if to make a final climax to the day's performance, Bob, the head ghost, started a small bon-fire up stairs, and he and the other ghosts piled all the chairs in the parlor one on top of the other, until they made a pile about six feet in height, when, as if in sport, they pulled out those underneath, letting all the others fall to the floor with a crash.

On Tuesday morning when the author took his seat at the breakfast table, he placed the sugar bowl lid beside his plate, so that he might have his eyes on it. In a second it disappeared and fell, in exactly eight minutes by the clock, from the ceiling, a distance of fully twenty feet from the table. The ghosts got under the table, as on the previous morning, and were so obliging as to produce any sounds called for, such as an exact imitation of the sawing of wood, of drumming and of washing on a wash board. During the morning several knives were thrown at him; a large crock of salt was taken from the kitchen dresser and placed on the dining room table; the tea kettle was taken from the stove by one of the ghosts and placed out in the yard, as was also the beefsteak, pan and all, which was frying on the stove; and, after dinner, the table was upset. During the afternoon, while in the parlor, the author made the acquaintance of all the ghosts,—Bob Nickle, the chief ghost; Maggie Fisher, another ghost almost as bad as Bob; Peter Cox, a quiet old fellow of very little use as a ghost, because he never tries to break chairs, etc.; Mary Fisher, (who says she is Maggie's sister) Jane Nickle and Eliza McNeal. The three last are "no good" as ghosts, as all they do is stalk about the house and occasionally upset something. As there are only six ghosts all told, and they were all present, the author asked them numerous questions, all of which were answered by loud knocks on the floor or on the wall, just as he requested—all seeming anxious to converse. The first question the author asked was:

"Have you all lived on the earth?"

A.—"Yes."

Q.—"Have you seen God?"

A.—"No."

Q.—"Are you in heaven?"

A.—"No."

Q.—"Are you in hell?"

A.—"Yes."

Q.—"Have you seen the devil?"

A.—very loud—"Yes."

Many other questions were answered, but the answers are not worth repeating.

At the conclusion of the interview, one of the ghosts threw the author's bottle of ink from the table to the floor, spilling the contents on the carpet.

The next day as the author and Esther were entering the parlor, both saw a chair fall over and instantly jump up again. Neither the author nor Esther were within five feet of the chair at the time.

During the whole of the next day the ghosts stuck pins into Esther's person. These pins appeared to come out of the air and the author pulled about thirty from various parts of her body during the day. In the afternoon the family cat was thrown a distance of five feet by one of the ghosts, and almost had a fit from fright. She remained in the yard for the balance of the day, and ever afterwards while in the house seemed to be on the lookout for ghosts; possibly she saw and heard them on several occasions afterwards, for her tail often became quite large, as cats' tails always do when they are frightened or angry, after which she would leave the house in a hurry. The author saw Esther coming down stairs late in the afternoon, and when she had reached the hall a chair from his room came down after her. The only other person in the cottage at the time was Olive, and she was at that instant in the kitchen.

On June 26th, two or three matches fell from the ceiling at the author's feet. Being a great smoker, he requested the ghosts to throw down a few more, which they did. He would simply say, "Bob, I would like a few matches, if you please." When down they would come from the ceiling. Forty-five were thrown during the day, and on another day during the afternoon forty-nine fell to the floor.

It must be remembered that all the manifestations witnessed by the author took place in the broad light of day, and that the only other persons present were the various members of the family.

On June 28th, the sound of a trumpet was heard by the author and all the family. It continued to be blown about the house from early morning until late in the evening. The sound was very distinct and was at times close to their ears. Late in the evening "Bob" let the trumpet fall in one of the rooms. It is composed of some metal very similar to German silver, and is now in the possession of the author, who intends to place it in a museum on his return to the United States. Where the ghosts got it no one knows. It had never been seen in Amherst, so far as had been ascertainable, until it fell upon the floor, and its true origin will doubtless always remain a mystery.

It is hardly necessary that the author should weary the reader with a minute account of the manifestations produced by these ghosts during his residence of six weeks in the haunted house, he could easily fill a book containing twice the number of pages that this one does, with an account of what was done by the ghosts alone, without mentioning the name of a single living individual except Esther Cox; but I suppose the reader, by this time, is ready to cry "**quantum sufficit**." So by referring to a few more facts, he will end this chapter.

One afternoon, while Esther was out walking, she called on Rev. R.A. Temple. During the visit he prayed with her, and also advised her to pray for herself. On her return to the cottage, one of the ghosts, either Bob or Maggie, cut her on the head with an old bone from the yard, and a moment afterwards stabbed her in the face with a fork.

While the author lived in the house, scarcely a day passed that some article was not thrown by the ghosts. They would often steal small articles and keep them secreted—Heavens only knows where—for days at a time, and then unexpectedly let them fall in one of the rooms, to the amazement of every one. In that way, shoes and stockings, knives, forks and other articles too numerous to mention would be missed, sometimes for weeks, and on one occasion some copper coins were taken from Dan's pocket and placed upon the author's knee.

It was a common thing for the ghosts to throw knives at the author, but fortunately they were all dull and he was never cut; he was, however, often struck by small articles, never sufficiently hard, however, to draw blood. During his stay in the house, Esther often went into a state very similar to the mesmeric sleep, during which she talked with people invisible to all present; among others, her dead mother. On coming out of this strange state she always said she had been to heaven among the angels.

On several occasions, Bob, the head ghost, tormented her so at night that it was with difficulty she could remain in bed. On one particular occasion the author was called up by Dan at midnight so that he might behold for himself what was going on. After dressing, he went into Esther's room, and was horrified by the sight which met his gaze. There, upon the bed, lay the poor, unhappy girl swollen to an enormous size, her body moving about the bed as if Beelzebub himself were in her, while between her gasps for breath she exclaimed in agonizing sobs: "Oh, my God, I wish I were dead! I wish I were dead!"

"Oh, don't say that, Esther," plead Olive, "don't say that."

"Now, Mr. Hubbell," said Jane to the author, "you see how much she suffers."

"Yes, I see," said Hubbell, "but let us endeavor to hold her, so that this fiend cannot move her about the bed, and then, perhaps, she will not suffer so much." So Dan and himself tried to hold her so that she could not be moved, but in vain.

"Well," said Hubbell, "one ghost is certainly stronger than two men. Are you sure nothing can be done to relieve her?"

"No," replied Olive, "Dr. Caritte has tried everything without affording her the slightest relief. Medicine has no more effect on her than water."

Jane, Olive, Dan and the author remained up with her for about three hours, during which time she continued to move about the bed, after which the ghost left her and she sank from sheer exhaustion into a state of lethargy. She had several attacks of this kind during the author's residence in the cottage, and on one occasion she was seen by Mr. G.G. Bird, Mr. Jas. P. Dunlap, Mr. Amos Purdy and several ladies; on another occasion by Dr. E.D. McLean, Mr. Fowler and Mr. Sleep.

Towards the latter part of July the manifestations became so powerful that it was no longer safe to have Esther in the house. Fires were continually being started, the walls were being broken by chairs, the bed clothes pulled off in the day time, heavy sofas turned upside down, knives and forks thrown with such force that they would stick into doors, food disappeared from the table, finger marks became visible in the butter, and, worse than all, strange voices could be heard calling the inmates by name in the broad light of day. This was too much; if the ghosts continued to gain in strength they would take possession of the house and all in it, for there were six ghosts, and only five persons in the flesh all told, as follows: Dan, Olive, Jane, Esther and the author, not, of course, counting the two children—William Cox and John Teed having left the house before Esther went to St. John, literally driven away by ghosts.

There was but one remedy, and that was that Esther Cox should leave the house even though her sisters loved her dearly. Simple hearted village maiden! Fate decreed that she should be torn from their home, but not from their hearts for the simple reason that her room was far more agreeable than her company.

So one morning, after packing up all her worldly possessions, she kissed the little boys, embraced her sisters, shook hands with the rest, bade them all farewell, and departed never to return.

CHAPTER VI

CONCLUSION

Esther is living with her friends the Van Amburgh's, on their farm in the woods. The ghosts do not torment her now. With the Van Amburghs she has a quiet, peaceful home. One thing is certain, if she returned to Dan's cottage manifestations would, in a short time, become as powerful as ever, and Heaven only knows where the matter would end.

The author went to see her at the farm, On August 1st, 1879, and found her making a patch-work quilt, on which she stopped working every few minutes to play with the little children. She informed him that she read her Bible regularly every day, and was contented and happy. Before departing he advised her to pray earnestly that she might never again, be possessed by devils. She promised to take his advice. So hoping that her prayers would be answered, he bade her farewell forever.

In Dan's little cottage all is now harmony and peace. Pretty Jane still tends her plants with loving care. Olive works as hard as ever, and so does honest Dan. And there may they reside for years to come, enjoying the blessings which the virtuous always receive from the hands of Providence.

Reader, a word. This account of the "Haunted House," in which Esther Cox suffered so much, and the author had such a remarkable experience, is no fanciful creation of the imagination, but really what it is claimed to be,—"A True Ghost Story."